INTERNATIONAL TRADE USING THE CLOUD

A. Luis Flores-Galea

ISBN: 1480250309
ISBN-13: 9781480250307

DEDICATION

This book is dedicated to my wife Anna. We will be soon living our dream. Take it for granted.

CONTENTS

ACKNOWLEDGMENTS

I want to acknowledge the people that encouraged me to start writing this book, especially my teachers at ISEAD, and also the people that have taught me the importance of the international trade and the application of the ICT to business, José Manuel Campa, Rolf Campos, Evgeny Káganer and Julián Villanueva, teachers at IESE Business School.
I want to thank many people I had the chance to discuss this book, including my family and my mates at IESE. I hope you will benefit from their knowledge through reading this book.

INTRODUCTION

This book aims to illustrate and summarize systematically how the technology available in the telecommunications framework can provide solutions to many of the great classics of international trade issues, such as those associated with logistics, control and efficiency of the sales departments and other aspects that directly or indirectly impact on the profit and loss account of the company. The good and adequate use of communications solutions can be far less expensive for the company than any other policies based on traditional perspectives.

Perhaps the greatest evidence in the use of telecommunications, joint with the information systems or Information Technology (*IT*), is in the field of electronic billing and payment media. To this we have dedicated the chapter 3, which also shows the latest trends in this field.

In the fourth chapter, a quick guide for applying the tools and solutions available in the

ICT sector to any Small and Medium Enterprise (*SME*) has been included. The objective is to provide one of the easiest way to optimize their business processes through them in a practical manner.

In the last section, we have tried to highlight some ideas and business opportunities that, after the analysis of the needs presented in the previous chapters, may represent some technological niches with high returns in the short to medium term.

Last but not least, a section with several links to webpages related to some cloud-based applications has been included in order to provide you with useful information for starting up the process of moving your global business into the cloud.

Remember this book aims to be an introductory guide to the cloud for those who are non-technical people and want to understand the principles of this widespread technology especially for the international trade. Sometimes you will find the content easy to understand and some others you will think it is getting a bit tough. The true is the cloud involves highly complex applications and solutions, and it is not necessary to understand the last detail of a solution.

CHAPTER 1. COMMUNICATION TECHNOLOGY FOR IMPROVING BUSINESS EFFICIENCY ABROAD

Probably one of the biggest concerns for a company when considering the step of internationalization is to know, with the highest level of detail, who their customers overseas are expected to be. Usually the business structure and resources for marketing and sales in the foreign country will be one of the pillars of the new strategy.

This chapter discusses some points of great importance when evaluating which technologies and services should be considered in the internationalization project of any company. Also, many of the points mentioned here also apply to already established international businesses, seeking to reduce operating costs and barriers that arise intrinsically to existing geographical distances when operating in the global market.

CURRENT SCENARIO

According to the study published by Darrell Rigby of Bain & Co. in 2007, companies are largely in agreement with the following assumptions:

❖ The corporate culture is as important as the strategy for the business success.

❖ Computer systems can be a significant competitive advantage.

❖ Innovation is more important than cost reduction for the long-term success.

❖ The consolidation and division of back-office work improve the quality and reduce the cost.

❖ The products and practices that respect the environment should be an important part of the mission of the company.

❖ Innovation can be significantly boosted by

collaborating with third parties, including competitors.

❖ An increasing percentage of the products and services of the company behave like commodities.

In this report, the changing trends regarding the tools used by companies to improve their business are also reflected. It can be said that strategic planning is the most important tool since 1996 and that the star is the scene is the **CRM** (*Customer Relationship Management*) application. The target for implementing a CRM solution is to register all interaction with customers in a database, including orders, invitations to events, marketing and commercial campaigns, complaints, data of contact persons and any other information that will help anyone in the company to know who and how each customer is. Customer segmentation has become more important within the time, while the *benchmarking*, or analysis of the company based on a model which copies the competition one with some or any adaptations, has declined slightly in importance.

In conclusion, we can state that the **information flow** in the organization, using certain tools, contributes to its success, and to facilitate other tasks also closely linked to business success, such as innovation, consolidation of tasks and collaboration between companies. This agility, required to have the information consolidated in the minimum number of sources at the time it is available for the largest number of users, is provided by the modern communications systems, integrated within the IT infrastructure of the company.

All these premises, which are important for any business, become more necessary in the international arena, where geographical distances make the schedule matching for several countries difficult, cultural differences often curb human interaction and the ignorance of the rest of the organization by individuals from a remote site makes them feel lost frequently, wasting their potential to achieve the maximum efficiency in management, due to this lack of information.

PROCESSES

It is useful to recall the processes that every company must take to start internationalization, in order to study how to improve them using communications technologies and the cloud. These processes may be summarized as:

❖ Detection of needs and definition of the local supply

❖ Target market segmentation

❖ Business action plan: subsidiaries, offices, distributors and agents

❖ Quality control and customer satisfaction

We will see next to what extent the use of the latest communications technologies can support the increased productivity of the people involved in the development of the processes above.

Detection of Needs and Definition of the Local Supply

As for the needs of assessment, it is common to use a more or less comprehensive market research, and a comparative study of the target culture with local or other countries where the company has already started to export, and detect adjustments in terms of products and services to be offered in the new country.

A more modern approach, conducted by many companies nowadays, especially those with low budget and those which have large resources to launch campaigns globally, is to use the **social networks** to test the market first. They thus get a fully updated market study on a sufficiently large population. Based on this technique, which a priori may seem rather rudimentary and unscientific, many companies specialized in this, like Corbax, under the concept of **SMO** (*Social Media Optimization*) have flourish.

TARGET MARKET SEGMENTATION

This work is a purely strategic task that does not require telecommunications systems to be done. However, some very top level IT-based solutions associated with business intelligence are involved on it, such as the *Data Mining* and *Data Warehouse*. **Data Mining** consists of getting to certain market segmentation parameters from the data stored in the database of the company's CRM system. For example, the percentage of individuals who use a particular product on a regular basis against those who do so sporadically. The **Data Warehouse** is a higher-level solution that draws on different *data mining* operating in the company, and other inputs given by experts in market strategy and the sales forecasts provided by the sales department, to venture a 'future picture' of the company and thus suggest the optimum adaptation of all processes to align the strategy in that direction.

Business Action Plan

It is known that the commercial activity in foreign trade can be done in many ways. The most frequent are the openings of branches quite independently in terms of management, sites linked to the staff headquarters, dealers who buy and resell the products to local customers and sales agents, whose only contractual relationship with the company is that regulating the commissions paid for the sales referred to the agent and certain protective covenants and obligations contained in the commercial agency contract.

At this point, the use of telecommunications systems is crucial, both voice and data, fixed or mobile, allowing cloud solutions to operate. The following are the most relevant services for each of the four scenarios listed above:

Subsidiary

A subsidiary should benefit from contracting the telecommunications services locally in the country, by having its own legal entity in that country, as this will offer considerable cost savings. The three most important criteria to consider in this case are the following:

❖ The ability of the Internet Services Provider (ISP) to provide an International VPN service, to interconnect the subsidiary with the headquarters and the other subsidiaries, with the maximum guarantee of security and data traffic bandwidth.

❖ An attractive price for international calls and roaming, especially in mobile telephony. Today it is possible to find some companies offering international flat rates for mobile data, such as Podsystem. Podsystem already has a European flat rate for a mobile Internet connection, at a price much less prohibitive than traditional carriers, especially some years ago.

❖ International calls from landlines with minimum cost, using carriers offering IP telephony services. IP telephony is a service based on using the Internet connection of the company to send the actual content of the phone call, so you do not need to book a telephone circuit that calls (and gets billed) for the entire duration, but it travels coupled with other information that enters and leaves the company to the Internet. Cost cutting is dramatic, mostly for international calls.

For companies with a relatively small size, where an installation of the IP telephony service by the operator involves a high investment in equipment and licenses, penalizing the TCO of the solution and making not viable the IP infrastructure versus using traditional telephony, there is an alternative, gaining followers daily by the company **Skype**. Skype is software that is installed on the employee's PC or smartphone and allows her to make calls using it, processed through the same Internet connection, free of charge as long as the destination is another computer with Skype, anywhere in the world. There are also WiFi or Bluetooth-based wireless terminals that allow Skype to connect to the service without forcing the user to sit in front of her PC. With the Skype software for smartphones, the user can make calls through it from her own mobile phone, whilst an Internet connection is available. All this equipment will be always cheaper than the integration of an IP telephony solution by an operator if the subsidiary has fewer than 10 employees.

Local Office

For the opening of an office with a small staff —typically less than 25 people—, the typical structure is to have there people from sales, marketing, customer service, technical support and, eventually, some temporary displaced employees, sent to that country to perform certain local actions, business development or global research for the company.

Here, besides using Skype services to reduce the cost of calls to the headquarters and negotiate good rates on international calls, Internet connection and *roaming* with ISPs and carriers, the use of remote collaboration services, especially videoconferencing, will be highly interesting.

The videoconferencing equipment often use the Internet connection of the site to transmit high-resolution images and high-fidelity sound, but are usually quite expensive. The most known suppliers of videoconferencing equipment are currently Cisco-Tandberg and Polycom. These two brands offer first-class equipment for videoconference, including the so called immersive presence rooms, offering an almost real meeting experience. There are other low-entry solutions, like those provided by Radvision and Vidyo. These solutions can be hardware-based, but they also provide software for PC, tablets and smartphones, at a much lower cost than the traditional ones.

If it will be necessary frequent dialogue between the staff at the headquarters and the people at the local office, especially with clients or important people outside the organization, investment in these solutions will be more than justified and will provide the company with one of the most powerful tool based on the cloud. If, however, there will only be needed some low-resolution images to perform more personal meetings among employees, it will be advisable to equip PCs with *webcams*. The Skype program and many others like Microsoft 'Live Messenger' will allow conducting video calls using this far-cheaper technology. There are webcams in the market for less than $20 and many laptops, including the popular ultra-light PCs called *netbooks,* come with a webcam integrated over the screen, giving the user even a greater simplicity for usage.

Distributors

Dealers are like regular customers for all purposes so there will be limitations in integrating communications solutions with them for taking the best benefits from a cloud-based solution. However, there are useful solutions to solve this issue, like Electronic Data Interchange (**EDI**) protocol. EDI is intended to facilitate the transfer of billing information and orders among companies. In section 3.5, we will see something more about its chances. Basically, it is a language or code that allows several business management systems (called ERP, standing for 'Enterprise Resource Planning'), usually different from each other, to exchange information under a standard basis.

Regarding the use of integrated applications, the company can make available to its dealers real-time information about the available stock for each reference of products, and **self-service** solutions, where the dealer enters the orders or the required information associated with its business directly in the enterprise systems, through a PC or a mobile device. The technical infrastructure for providing this service is called **extranet**. An extranet is another cloud solution and consists of a secure connection, where the dealer must have been recorded by the exporting company and validate its login credentials each time he access the platform, being possible to do that from any device connected to the Internet on any part of the world.

Agents

Agents usually maintain enough independence from the operation of the supplier, so this kind of agreement does not require too much movement of information for the daily business. In this case, the exporter company will typically provide promotional and operating stuff via **e-mail** or an extranet based on ***web services***. This means that access to the extranet will be held by the agent itself through the Internet browser, without installing any additional software. This is also called a public cloud solution because anyone can access the application just by using his own Internet connected device.

As the agents may work for multiple companies simultaneously, the company should provide them with a simple, **little intrusive** service to facilitate their work with our company systems. In this case, it is also very important to take into account the **language barrier**.

For telephony, the only way to reduce the high cost of calls —observe that we won't be able to benefit from the higher discounts the carriers usually apply for internal calls to the companies because the agent will have an independent telephony contract— will be convincing them to use *software* like Skype. This solution is, in fact, a de facto standard worldwide, and also free, so it will also allow the agents to get the same benefit from using it with many other partners they represent.

QUALITY CONTROL AND CUSTOMER SATISFACTION

The quality control is probably one of the most critical issues in international trade. Firstly because you have to match the quality standards to the areas or countries involved and, secondly because due to the large distance between the different locations, it will be quite costly to send staff to do direct inspection, monitoring and identification of possible improvements in the local processes. It will also be inefficient to devote local staff to this work in each venue, unless there is a large activity volume and relevance in the overall income of the company.

There are some tools for **managing PCs remotely**, and some tools for doing the same with certain **mobile devices**. So far, the only platform including remote management for mobile devices natively is **BlackBerry**, although some other brands like Nokia and Microsoft have put solutions in the market for the same object, but far expensive. These are justified just in case of the existence of subsidiaries with high pools of devices, wanting to consolidate processes globally to reduce costs.

The quality control is usually performed by asking feedback the client itself, but it is also very valuable to open a suggestion box for the employees and establish an interdepartmental *feedback* process, which recognize potential areas for improvement.

To achieve feedback fast and efficiently, information systems of the company have an active role in the work to simplify and streamline its management. Additionally, we can also define an additional tool category, where the feedback is provided by the product itself. This is called **traceability** and consists of knowing what phases, with its origin, destination and transit time, each unit or batch of product sold is passing.

Thanks to the wireless data transmission technologies, such as **GPRS**, to geographical location systems like **GPS** and the possibility to integrate certain **ultra-reduced sized sensors** in the products, it is possible that the products themselves report their location, state and any data associated with the handling or delivery processes directly to the headquarters, constantly.

As the amount of data to be handled in this case will be overwhelming because all the information will be stores in real time in a central database, one has to realize that the important part is not to be able to access this information in full, but only save a little history of the last hours or days and shoot **alarms** at times unwanted situations are detected. When an alarm occurs, a small historic data series about what happened to that product just before and after the alarm will help study the reasons. It is, in fact, one of the best tools to identify a general problem or a failure in the process that need to be corrected.

CHAPTER 2. INTERNATIONAL LOGISTICS OPTIMIZATION THROUGH ICT

The information technology and communication (ICT) are now a key factor in the logistical organization of any multinational company. In this chapter, we analyze and illustrate possible solutions that will help them improve their logistics tasks, especially in the international arena.

REQUIREMENTS ADDED TO THE DECISION OF CHOOSING THE SITES

A key point to take advantage of the benefits of ICT for the logistics sector is to ensure that the logistics centers of the company are located in areas or countries covered by suppliers of the Internet access services. Thus, it would be advisable to check with the major telecom operators in the country where the matrix is located about coverage of services in the different countries we are considering for logistical operation, and include these aspects in the overall assessment for the choice of location of the logistics centers.

INVENTORY MANAGEMENT

Inventory control, with the highest possible level of accuracy, is probably the issue that mostly affects the cost of international logistics. For this concern, it is recommended to install a centralized system which take care of that, communicated in real time with all stores and outlets, where all the inputs and outputs of goods in warehouses are immediately registered, on the one hand, and sales and returns, on the other.

At a technical level, these solutions require from global **Virtual Private Networks (VPN)**, to communicate all centers (warehouses and retail outlets) with the control center, quickly and safely. A VPN is a network that connects several remote points using each one's Internet connection, but with a special feature: the information is encrypted and only the users of that network have access to communicate with each other, so no one else can access the information being exchanged. The latter task is performed by a particular method of credential validation, which prevents any other individual 'see' these connections from the Internet.

REDUCTION OF THE SAFETY STOCK

This is a very critical point for many multinationals as it represents a high cost. The safety stock grows with the uncertainty associated with the product's demand, and it grows with the square root of the delivery time —the time since the customer orders the product until it is delivered—, and with the square root of the number of options the product has, along with the deviation produced in the sales forecasts.

Several techniques related to communications

are applicable to reduce this uncertainty.

First, by using a centralized **CRM** tool, as seen before. It is possible to record all the information related to the company's customers in each country, which includes not only the orders generated, but also the forecast of business opportunities, estimated by the sales floor, and budgets given to potential customers (*prospects*). This will allow much more accurately refine the estimate of sales for each period and for each type of products, which will benefit the reduction of the safety stock. A very useful kind of tools based in the cloud offers the possibility to generate **budgets** *online* through a tablet or smartphone so that the benefit is twofold: first, the customer can get an exact quote with all the references she is interested in buying, personalized with their precise discount levels, estimated delivery time, etc. On the other hand, the budget can be registered automatically as potential sale in the central database, associated with a probability of closing, assigned by the sales rep *on-site,* or beyond believable, according to historical ratios of closing operations, which take account of the customer, the geographical area and the products offerings. This is largely related to the *business intelligence* systems, already seen in a previous section.

A second derivative that allows reduction of the safety stock, by reducing the times of the supply chain is also favored by the fact of having all the **information associated with a potential order centrally located**. The scheduling of the production chain can then be made on the basis of statistical data calculated much more accurately and adjusted than those obtained from the market trends. This will help reduce lead times, on average. This premise does not apply to products whose demand and features are very stable over time, but it will be a very significant improvement in the case of products with a short period of obsolescence, that must share resources in a factory or assembly line.

For example, suppose that the assembly line 'A' assembles high-definition flat-screen-television parts (HDTV) and 19 inches computer displays (19TFT). Based on the sales history of the company, it is known that, for every 19TFT sold, 2 HDTVs are also sold. Therefore, at the time to manufacture on the basis of having a worldwide stock, a 19TFT is produced for every 2 HDTV. If you have a sales forecasting system as seen above, where you can register the budgets made to customers and closing probabilities associated with high accuracy, we can predict at some moment that sales of 19TFT will begin to fall in the next month, for example, at the time the 21 inches displays (21TFT) begin to grow, assembled by the assembly line 'B'. So, it will be recommended to modify the assembly 'A' production plan to assemble more HDTV and less 19TFT.

By applying this technique, we will reduce the delivery time of products and, therefore, the number of units required in stock since the assembly line introduces less inertia in the production system.

Finally, the possibility of having a global inventory management updated at each instant allows the **launch of a delivery order to the optimal warehouse** at any time. Thus, it is possible to minimize the safety stock at each store location and manage fewer product options in each area because it will be possible to release the order to another store that has less common options for that area. Although this may increase the delivery time for a product in the case of rare options over usual delivery time, it helps increase customer satisfaction in general terms as there will be able to publish a globally comprehensive catalog of options. The point is that the reduction in stocks costs will increase the competitiveness of the company at the same time.

TRANSPORTATION MANAGEMENT

Transportation is another important activity of international logistics, not so much related to direct economic resources consumption as in terms of complex planning needs, which will result in an overall reduction of logistics costs. It is, therefore, very important to ensure its optimization, reducing transit times, simplifying and optimizing transport invoices routes and resources to minimize the impact this item has on the total cost of the product.

There is some equipment dedicated to **tracing** the goos in the market, that is, to record when, where and how an order is traveling. This makes it possible to perform a posteriori analysis to optimize resources, or even in real time, to detect possible contingencies and make decisions as quickly as possible.

There are several technologies that are used nowadays to get these benefits:

❖ Thanks to the Global Positioning satellite System (**GPS**), the load can be equipped with a device to record its position on any point on Earth and the exact time of each measurement.

❖ This equipment can also have integrated **impact, orientation or rotation sensors**, to know if a package has being knocked on a certain scale (measured in 'G') or has been targeted in the wrong direction, and when this occurred.

❖ A **temperature sensor** will be vital to

ensure the preservation of the food cold chain, and to trigger alarms in case of flammable goods or transportation of live animals.

❖ All this information can be recorded for a later analysis or transmitted in real time via a **GPRS connection** through mobile carrier networks worldwide. This will be possible only in land transport (road and rail) and also in areas close to ports, but not in the case of air transportation.

As you have seen, the benefit of using these technologies in transport can be useful in the face of negotiating transit insurance costs, and to determine the levels of the final product quality, influenced by inclement or manipulation suffered during the transportation.

ORDER PROCESSING

The order processing is a logistic function quite often stated as a source of human errors. The reason is simple: it is a fairly mechanical and monotonous task, no very pleasant for the people involved, thus there will obviously occur absence of references in an order, or misreading of product codes.

There are widely implemented technologies such as the use of bar codes, and their readers, to minimize the number of reading code errors, but it is even possible to go a step further. The labels known as **RFID** (*Radio Frequency IDentifiers*) are small plastic labels which adhere to the product in the manufacturing process, or to the packaging afterwards. These labels are able to obtain energy from the environment for delivering a short message with some information about the product (its reference code and other properties, that other devices can receive and process. Thus, a receiver located at a the entrance of a warehouse is able to identify the products entering and leaving the place, automatically. Another device placed at the doors of a truck's cargo can also identify which products are being loaded and unloaded, and even a supermarket box will be able to check a shopping cart without having any items removed from it.

RFID solutions are currently available at affordable prices, both in terms of equipment and the necessary integration services, usually carried out by engineering companies specializing in this field.

INTEGRATED SUPPLY CHAIN

An undeniable success of ICT for the logistics management in a company, especially in the global environment, is the possibility of creating an integrated supply chain management, so that the set of customer orders configures the manufacturing plant scheduling itself. Although this does not apply 100% in consumer goods, where you need the product at the point of sale to let the consumer pick it at the very moment he formalizes the order, it is widespread in other sectors, such as automotive and computers —the case of Dell Computers. This is the technique called 'just in time'.

This technique is based on the intense record of time throughout the production and assembly chain, together with a comprehensive quality control that minimizes the number of errors and defective products. This way, you can give the customer an accurate and short-enough delivery date, supporting in closing the sale, with the advantage of allowing choices for each product.

ELECTRONIC MANAGEMENT OF WAYBILLS, BILLS OF LADING AND TIR

At present, there already exist companies that provide IT-based solutions (hardware and software) suitable for **digitizing all documents** associated to an expedition, so any employee of the company can access them from anywhere in the world, even at the same time than others. Some companies, such as the German *SER-Solutions,* have gone a step further, creating an automated system for processing incoming documents, called *'Inbound Center'.* It automatically analyzes the new incoming documents, classifies them and selects the appropriate file to archive them, without any human intervention.

Government authorities are also implementing computerized techniques for the administrative procedures associated to export and import, reducing the transfer of information on paper and making the procedures of sending and consulting documents easier and faster as all the information is available on the *web*. Thus, some tax agencies have a service for the data exchange under the Electronic Data Interchange standard called EDIFACT, allowing online clearance of goods declarations NCTS-TIR. In fact, some agencies oblige to use this electronic procedure as the only way.

Using this new system, any company can send the information contained in the TIR to the competent customs authorities directly and free, without having to pay the services of a third party. In addition, by the use of this software application, the time required to manage each TIR book by such authorities greatly reduces, and this benefits not only the carrier, but the Administration, reducing the volume of their work dramatically, in the same proportion of the efficiency increases.

INFORMATION TO THE CUSTOMER

An important point about the technologies outlined in the two paragraphs above are the ability to provide comprehensive, or at least accurate, information to the customer receiving the goods. By this, the company fulfills the basic function of not frustrating the expectations and reduces the work load in the customer service department, resulting in lower operating costs.

BUSINESS INTELLIGENCE

This concept is gaining significant importance over time. It is a continuous process, which analyzes the performance of the business to determine what changes are needed to increase productivity.

It is clearly evident that, if our company has all information provided by the transport layout equipment and order processing in a centralized data warehouse, it will be easy to apply some **algorithms** for drawing conclusions from the analysis of these data. This task is known as *data mining* and is vital to the major multinational companies, where the variables are many, and complexity of the logistics systems are high.

CHAPTER 3. LATEST COMMUNICATIONS TECHNOLOGIES APPLIED TO BILLING AND INTERNATIONAL PAYMENT METHODS

This chapter provides some technology solutions that, applied to the billing process of a company where international actors are involved, by the person who buys or sells, through the B2B or the B2C models, can improve response times and reduce operating costs of that process.

INTERNATIONAL STAGE

It is shown that the application of e-commerce technologies to the international billing processes involve cost cutting in several aspects:

❖ For purchases, by reducing the mark-up

for suppliers and increasing the market transparency.

❖ During the transaction, by using information systems integrated with the production chain of the company.

❖ In the supply chain, by automating the purchasing process.

Although e-commerce is steadily gaining popularity, it does not represent the total international operations, so it is also necessary to pay attention to the traditional process of buying and selling, based on the exchange of paper documents.

Below are the different mechanisms for billing and payment methods that can be used to increase the efficiency of the process when we are in a multinational environment.

ELECTRONIC BANKING

It is now possible to manage a bank account through a secure Internet connection. The majority of the banks offer this service internationally, sometimes for free and other charging certain fees.

As for the use of electronic banking services or online banking as a means of payment, it can be said that its operation is very similar to the traditional ones because the bank provides the same '**virtual office**', where some kind of operations can be ordered. Each bank will offer a range of them as if we were at the window of a traditional office.

The main difference is that, whereas in the traditional method, they use the national ID card as the validation tool, virtual offices request the user name, password and a specific signature, which usually consists of a few keys that are provided to the user on a card and that only he should know.

The use of online banking is beneficial to both the exporter and importer. To the first, because he can check the record of a transaction without having to wait or move documents on paper to a bank branch. To the second, because he can make payments or process credits from their own office.

CREDIT CARDS

The study by American Express in May 2007 provided interesting data on the use the companies give to credit cards. It found that 25% of the companies make regular purchases via e-commerce, where card payment is mainly used. Additionally, credit cards offer the possibility of quick and easy access to funding, so they are used by many individuals and businesses today, although interest rates applied are much higher than those that can be achieved with other loan products, formalized directly with the credit department of a bank.

The use of credit cards in commerce requires some equipment called **POS** (Point Of Sale Terminal), which is a small calculator-shaped machine, networked to the bank through the landline in the customer's premise or via GPRS through the data connection of a mobile operator, and that reads the information from the card and the purchase made.

In the case of electronic commerce, the bank will provide the customer with software or a set of commands for incorporation into his webpage. The latter is known as a **Virtual POS** because this software will perform the same task as the traditional POS, but without installing any reader device. The buyer will enter the credit card data during the order process directly from his computer, and some packet of information will be sent to the credit card validation authority to make the purchase.

PAYPAL

PayPal is an American company, currently owned by eBay, which allows money transfers between users who own a simple email account. PayPal allows its customers to open an account linked to that email address, and it is possible to maintain a balance in the desired currency —or multiple currency—, make payments to other

PayPal users or receive payments from them. If the user enables some additional functionality in his profile, it also permits the processing of payment by credit card requests.

PayPal is undoubtedly the main economic transaction manager for B2C e-commerce, given the simplicity to make payments: you only need an email account, then the payer can choose to pay by credit card whether he does not have a PayPal account or use its own PayPal account for the payment.

However, PayPal warns they are not a bank, so in B2B commerce is not really spread yet, due to the lack of protection from possible disagreements in transactions.

The truth is that the boom it has had in recent times is the result of simplicity for electronic payment transactions in all markets. In the case of international business, this advantage becomes even bigger.

EDI

The EDI, or Electronic Data Interchange, is a mechanism that allows the interconnection of different business systems, such as ERP or CRM, to conduct a trade or exchange of any information. There are several standard protocols that establish how to communicate this information, like the widespread standard for the public administration **EDIFACT** (*Electronic Data Interchange for Administration, Commerce and Transport*) and other: XML, TXT ANSI ASC and X12, to mention a few.

EDIFACT is a UNO standard for exchanging business documents internationally, and there exists different classes for each business environment —retail, automotive, transportation, customs, etc— and for each country.

An example of an EDI solution is the based on the electronic billing platform, BizLayer, with high penetration in the tourism sector. This platform allows companies to manage their bills using the EDIFACT format and dump them to the BizLayer billing platform for subsequent management, in a simple and safe manner.

CHAPTER 4. NEW EXPORT OPPORTUNITIES BASED ON THE CLOUD

The information technology and communication, and more specifically the cloud-based solutions, are not just a useful tool to support the processes associated with a multinational, but also, given the high volume of business they generate for this reason, an international business object themselves. In fact, a lot of companies providing these services are multinationals as their main advantage usually lies in trying to get the information as far as possible in the shortest time, and this leads to cross the borders of their home country.

There are some business niches in the ICT market we can already consider as 'traditional', such as the operators of fixed and mobile telephony, as well as the Internet Service Providers (ISPs).

A market where there are still some gaps in the business is that of **security**: all the business transactions and the transfer of all information necessary for the internal management of a multinational enterprise require of significant safety levels as they are exposed to possible attacks from anywhere in the world, including espionage competition, terrorism, sabotage or simple *hacking*[1].

The **location-based services** (**LBS**) market is much less exploited. LBS solutions consist of the use of GPS technology, combined with sensors or events, to generate geo-referenced information, i.e. with a label, providing information about the place and time at which this information was generated. This information is passed onto the enterprise central systems through mobile data networks, usually the GPRS networks of mobile operators deployed

---

[1] Hacking is an attack on the information center of a company through the Internet, making non-destructive changes, for fun, challenge or protest actions. The authors of these acts, called *hackers*, are often mixed up —mostly by many journalists's ignorance—, with the attackers who try to destroy or steal information or systems, called *crackers*.

worldwide. There are numerous opportunities to cover the transport services for this information, specific sensor equipment manufacturing, device programming and integration of turnkey solutions based on all the elements above.

The application development and **peripheral integration** —like a ticket printer or bar code reader— are very close to this area. Good chances for new products can be found by integrating some peripherals with smartphones, mobile phones and tablets. These devices can serve as useful tools for running applications to execute orders, deliveries, inventories or authorizations, among others. Special mention in this case is for the **BlackBerry** brand, whose devices are highly prepared for this purpose, due to security granted to the information, the battery life and ease of use of the terminals.

CHAPTER 5. STRATEGIES FOR THE ADOPTION OF THE CLOUD BY SMES

It is fairly intuitive and logical that large corporations have more and better resources for the implementation of new solutions based on the cloud, and even almost any solution, that a small business or a sole proprietorship. However, it will be sometimes equally useful —or even more—, a company with few resources can get the most out of them. This statement not only applies to the field of the international trade, but also to the activity within the company.

This chapter is intended to be a first aid to illustrate a regular SME on where to go and what criteria to follow when implementing cloud-based solutions in their business processes.

ASSOCIATIONS AND CENTRAL PURCHASING

There are many SMEs associations, some of them local and others covering a bigger region. These associations can negotiate special prices on ICT and cloud services for its members, and it can become really advantageous for them. In other cases, the association contracts some resources to a supplier so they can be used on a shared basis by the member companies. These resources can be offered for free or at much more affordable prices than if every company had contracted them individually. An example of this is the training courses, highly needed in the field of the new technologies, because of the great cloud of new concepts that arise every day and also because they are not very intuitive to those unfamiliar with the industry.

An alternative to an association membership is to serve as a small power purchase among several small or medium-size companies. This is often the case in business parks and industrial estates. Thus, important synergies can be achieved in terms of availability of supply —there are suppliers that offer certain services only to companies of a minimum size— and promoting business relationships among companies in the park.

RECOMMENDED GUIDELINES

From a practical standpoint, it is advisable to follow these guidelines when considering adopting a strategy based on solutions in the cloud, in an SME:

❖ Hire an external expert for advice, who knows the market and the available technologies, to conduct a comprehensive analysis of the company's internal processes, capabilities and technological solutions best suited for her, prioritizing and evaluating the economic benefits that should result.

❖ Decide which solutions are to be implemented, based on eligibility criteria for the present company. For example, if we are to move the office, it will not make sense to invest in the deployment of a WiFi network in the current office, albeit it should mean a great benefit to the company in the short term.

❖ Find the most suitable suppliers to undertake projects. Interestingly, we are dealing with a highly globalized industry, therefore, providers are mostly multinationals. They tend to have a more or less local, both sales and customer support offices. The latter will be a vital aspect for an SME as it does not have enough resources to implement its own internal support department in most cases, and users must have a high-quality service and immediacy to resolve questions and issues.

❖ Hiring the services of an expert in finding funding for SMEs, both private and through subsidies. There are many companies and organizations that provide these services, with varying degrees of success.

❖ Finally, do not forget to set a criterion for evaluating and monitoring the benefits achieved. Do not implement a technology solution just because it is a current trend, but ask for a tailor made solution for your company. If the solution does not result enough profitably, adapt or substitute it for a better one. At this point, there are very few companies able to accurately track under its own power, joint to the fact that there is a shortage of consultants offering that kind of service, so that will probably be the most difficult task to undertake.

CHAPTER 6. CONCLUSIONS

As seen, the cloud-based applications, as well as the IT and communications solutions, not only have a very active role in the operations of companies with international presence today, but are very much an important part of the basic infrastructure for its operation and the heart of their business.

Companies that have taken full advantage of these new technologies have grown and established themselves in the global scope in an unprecedented way. Probably the best examples worldwide are the Spanish Inditex group, the American company Dell and the Japanese Toyota, all of them well studied in the most relevant business schools.

As a basic conclusion of we has read until now, it is quite important to go to experts in this field of solutions, who provide the greatest benefit to the specific needs of each company, especially in the early stages of the internationalization project. In consolidated companies, this premise will give way to the establishment of a separate department dedicated to this mission, that should stay in touch and be heard by the other departments of the company, and especially by the management.

Telecommunications and applications in the cloud are increasingly necessary daily tasks of consumers and businesses. Therefore, it is becoming necessary to integrate them into business processes and sales increasingly. The company that invests in these technologies will always be one step ahead of those which do not, on the steps of positioning and competitiveness.

CHAPTER 7. WEBS YOU SHOULD BE AWARE OF

In this chapter, I have included some lists with links you should visit in order to get interesting solutions and knowledge regarding applications in the cloud and communications technology involved.

❖ **www.google.com/apps**: a portal with all the enterprise tools of Google, in the cloud.

❖ **www.salesforce.com**: the most popular CRM solution in the cloud.

❖ **www.skype.com**: the most wide-spread software for VoIP using a PC or smartphone.

❖ **www.linkedin.com**: the first social network fully dedicated to professional links. Very useful for finding people in other countries.

❖ **www.paypal.com**: the easiest solution for global money interchange among end customers and companies.

❖ **www.tiemviewer.com**:   a   software-based

solution for managing remote PC, tablets and smartphones from another one.

❖ **www.logmein.com**: Another solution for remote PC management.

❖ **www.gtnexus.com**: A cloud-based platform for supply chain processes integration.

❖ **www.eyeos.com**: Cloud desktop for PC and mobile devices in order to facilitate applications and documents sharing and management in a global company.

❖ **www.vidyo.com**: an affordable video-conferencing solution based in the cloud.

❖ **www.yourconference.com**: a free conference calling service.

❖ **www.dropbox.com**: A cloud-based tool for sharing folders in multiple computers and mobile devices.

❖ **www.podsystem.com**: a carrier offering international flat fees for mobile Internet access.

❖ **www.surveymonkey.com**: a cloud-based tool for launching surveys to customers, employees or whatever easily.

CHAPTER 8. GLOSSARY

3G (Third Generation): term used for the generation of mobile communications systems including sound and data transmission at high speed.

4G: Fourth generation mobile technologies, allowing more speed. The most widespread one is LTE (see below).

ADSL (Asymmetric Digital Subscriber Line): data transmission technology over traditional landlines, where the speed of downloading information from the Internet is much greater than the uploading bandwidth.

Bandwidth: transmission medium capacity for transmitting data per unit of time. The higher the bandwidth the more data can be transmitted in a certain period. The typical unit is the kilobit or megabit per second (Kbps, Mbps). If you want to transmit video, you will need a minimum of several Mbps of bandwidth.

API (Application Programming Interface): set of functions, procedures and programming tools offered by a technology or manufacturer to others in order to allow them use their system easily. For example, Google provides an API for anyone to put a map or Google calendar on her own website.

Bit/byte: The bit is the smallest possible unit of information. It represents 'Yes/No' or 'True/False'. Using a bit stream, like the case of Morse code, one can form all the words that make up a program, an image, a web page and all the data types. A byte is a pack of 8 bits. This unit was created because the old computers processed bits in groups of 8. Thus, even today the byte is still used as a basic unit (notice the 'B' uppercase) for measuring the information processed in a computer, such as a file size, and the bit ('b' lowercase) for measuring the data transmitted through a transmission line (don't ask why…). As with the kilogram, there exist the kilobit (kb, 1,000 bits) and the megabit (Mb, 1,000 kb), but the kilobyte (kB) is equal to 1,024 bytes and the megabyte (MB) is equal to 1,024 kB. And so on and so forth. I guess you will have to read it again, slower...

Blog: personal website where someone writes a diary or posts on issues that arose her curiosity, and where people can leave some comments to each of them.

Bluetooth: short-range wireless technology that allows communication between small devices within the home, office or car. It works in free band frequencies, that means that we do not need to pay for the connection.

Digital Certificate: digital file that allows you to set the credentials of individuals, organizations and computers on the network. It prevents someone impersonate other person for critical operations on the Internet, such as banking.

Chat: Real-time online conversation established between two or more people. It basically occurs through texts, but it is also possible to use voice and video.

Cloud computing: it is a form where the user does not install the programs on her PC, but they are on the Internet, somewhere not necessarily known by her. Through a browser, the user can run the application, paying per use or on a monthly basis, without needing to buy the licenses.

CMS (Content Management System): application to manage the content of a website, without programming and formatting the pages. All the information is updated in a database, and it can be easily used by multiple people in the organization.

CRM (Customer Relationship Management): system that allows companies to manage all the information concerning its customers under a unified and digitized manner.

Data Warehouse: a system able to store a huge amount of information in order to perform further analysis afterwards.

DSL (Digital Subscriber Line): technology that offers a broadband data connection over the traditional landline. ADSL is a variety of DSL.

ERP (Enterprise Resource Planning): computer system for managing, in a unified way, all the resources of a company, including logistics, personnel, sales, stores, finance, etc.

Extranet: website that allows collaborators or remote employees connect to an organization's intranet on the Internet, from anywhere in the world.

Electronic invoice: digital file that is equivalent to the paper bill and has legal validity.

Firewall: hardware or software (program) responsible for the network's protection against intentional or accidental attacks from outside the organization or even different parts of the network in the company.

GPRS (General Packet Radio Service): system that allows to transmit data via the 2G network at low speed. Many BlackBerries use this service very efficiently to send and receive email, the same way the systems transmit the position of a GPS receiver. This technology is too slow to have a satisfactory experience surfing the Internet, as well as some other bandwidth-intensive services.

GPS (Global Positioning System): system

based on a network of 24 satellites that allows to obtain a receiver's highly accurate latitude, longitude and time anywhere in the world, beside the altitude (less accurately).

GSM (Global System Mobile): first digital cellular system. It is currently still in use and has shown high success in almost every country, in the world.

HSPA (High-Speed Packet Access): improved data service that allows 3G network speed equal to or greater than that of ADSL connections through a mobile phone line. If it only improves the downlink bandwidth it is called HSDPA and if it only improves the uplink bandwidth, it is called HSUPA.

HTML (HyperText Markup Language): standard language in which web pages are written.

HTTP (HyperText Transfer Protocol): Internet protocol used to send and receive web pages through the Internet.

IEEE (Institute of Electrical and Electronics Engineers): the biggest engineering association in the world, participated by electrical and electronic engineers, and responsible for publishing the standards concerning communication protocols and other related issues.

IMAP (Internet Message Access Protocol): a method for accessing the email messages on a server without needing download them to the user computer.

Intranet, Virtual Private Network (VPN): a network whose access is restricted to the people in an organization, by using the Internet as a part of the infrastructure. The information is encrypted when traveling on the Internet.

IP (Internet Protocol): a protocol used by all the devices and computers connected to the Internet to communicate with each other and transmit information.

ISP (Internet Service Provider): the companies that provide an Internet access.

Java: a programming language widely used in computers and mobile devices.

LAN (Local Area Network): cable network and the interconnection equipment needed (switches, routers) that connect a number of computers, printers and other equipment in a specific location (a building, a home, an office...).

LCD (Liquid Crystal Display): a glass colored by tinting point by point to form an image. This technology is being currently used by computers, mobile phones and tablets.

LED (Light Emitting Diode): microscopic device that emits light in one color without producing heat consuming, therefore, highly energy efficient.

LTE (Long Term Evolution): another name for the 4G mobile communications technology.

Mashup: a web application that uses resources from more than one source to create a new complete service.

MMS (Multimedia Messaging System): a service similar to the SMS messaging system, but with the ability to send images, video and sound, additionally to the text content.

MPLS (Multi-Protocol Label Switching): Internet protocol used in combination with TCP/IP protocol to allow sending voice, data, video and other types of data, without interfering with each other on the same connection. For example, if there is an ongoing phone conversation using voice over IP and someone starts to download a large file, no choppy voice will occur on the call because of the line is saturated with the file transmission.

NAS (Network Attached Storage): storage system that does not need to be connected to a computer, but appears as shared folders to all the users in a network.

Phishing: an attempt to acquire sensitive information fraudulently using some Internet tricks.

Pixel: the smallest unit in which a digital image is decomposed.

Podcast: an audio file that you can download from the Internet via a PC or mobile phone.

POP (Post Office Protocol): a protocol for downloading the email from a remote server to a

PC or mobile phone.

QWERTY: the standard distribution for the characters on a keyboard.

RFID (Radio Frequency IDentification): wireless system that allows you to read a little information, much like a bar code of a product, without having to point a device at him.

Router: device for connecting computers to a network.

RSS (Really Simple Syndication): protocol to share content easily between some readers and web pages.

SEO (Search Engine Optimization): task of adjusting the structure of information and web pages to make them appear in the top positions of the search results.

SMS (Short Message Service): Short Message Service for mobile phones.

SPAM: unsolicited electronic communication, usually email.

Spoofing: a technique to thieve someone's identity by using false e-mail sender addresses.

The target is to obtain some sensitive information such as passwords for access to bank accounts.

SSH (Secure Shell): protocol that facilitates secure communications between two systems.

SSL (Secure Socket Layer): process that manages the transactions made through Internet safely, for example, with a bank or the government.

TCP (Transmission Control Protocol): protocol used by computers connected to the Internet to organize the flow of traffic.

TCP / IP (Transmission Control Protocol / Internet Protocol): the set of protocols that make the Internet able to work.

UMPC (Ultra Mobile PC): laptop with several networking interfaces (WiFi, Bluetooth, 3G ...) and a very low weight. They usually cost much less than a traditional laptop, even less than half the price.

UMTS (Universal Mobile Telecommunications System): another name for 3G.

URL (Uniform Resource Locator): complete address that appears in the address bar of an Internet browser, that identifies a particular website.

Computer virus: program that automatically copies itself and which aims to alter the normal functioning of a computer, deleting information, making it run slower or stop working the operating system.

VoIP: Voice over IP, that is, using the Internet connection.

VPN (Virtual Private Network): see Intranet.

WAP (Wireless Application Protocol): protocol for simplified browsing pages for mobile phones.

Web: system that allows you to easily search, view and share content on devices connected to the Internet, using an URL and a page structure.

Web 2.0: applications and interactive websites that allow users to contribute data and interact with the different elements on the page, as are they were applications installed on their computers.

Webcam: a digital camera connected to a computer, allowing images capture for transmitting them over the Internet for video-chat.

Wi-Fi: short-range wireless system that connects computers, routers, mobile phones and other devices via a broadband connection. It has much higher consumption than Bluetooth, but permits several computers to connect with each other and with a much higher bandwidth.

Wiki: website whose pages can be edited by any volunteer and serves as a manual for something or a collection of concepts.

WiMAX (Worldwide Interoperability for Microwave Access): a medium range wireless technology that allows buildings be connected to each other, operating in a free band, without having to pay for using the connection.

ZigBee: specification of a set of wireless communication protocols to be used with low-power digital equipment.

BIBLIOGRAPHY

❖ Darrell   Rigby,   Bain   &   Co.
MANAGEMENT   TOOLS   AND
TRENDS   2007:
http://www.slideshare.net/whatidiscover
/management-tools-and-trends-2007

❖ Portal of credit cards: http://www.tarjeta-credito-online.es

❖ Wilson, M.T. HOW TO ORGANIZE
AND LEAD A SALES TEAM. Deusto
editions, 2001. ISBN 84-234-1889-8.

❖ Sainz de Vicuña Ancín, J.M. THE
MARKETING PLAN IN PRACTICE.
ESIC editions, 2002. ISBN 84-7356-298-4.

❖ Monsoriu, M. MANUAL OF SOCIAL
NETWORKING. Creaciones Copyright
editions, 2009. ISBN 978-84-96300-75-0.

❖ Luque, J. VIDEOCONFERENCING.
Creations Copyright editions, 2008. ISBN

978-84-96300-66-8.

❖ Flores-Galea, A. L. GETTING THE MOST OF YOUR BLACKBERRY. Creaciones Copyright editions, 2008. ISBN 978-84-96300-71-2.

❖ Flores-Galea, A. L. 50 TIPS FOR SUCCESS IN YOUR BUSINES. Creaciones Copyright editions, 2011. ISBN 978-84-92779-78-9.

ABOUT THE AUTHOR

 Antonio Luis Flores-Galea obtained his Master's degree in Communications Engineering in 2001, followed by a Master's degree in Electronics Engineering, in 2003, becoming one of the rare people with double Engineering degree in that two-year period.

His first job was as a teacher and researcher in the University of Seville (Spain), working on several projects related to natural disaster monitoring systems and circuit design for Internet over the power grid connections.

In 2003, he joined HP as Account Manager for the Corporate IT division, after having attended the Sales University in the firm. In 2005, he started working in a similar position in Orange, the biggest carrier in Europe, where he was designed for developing and implementing the sales strategy regarding the mobile data solutions for the corporate accounts in Spain in 2007.

In 2009, Luis got his Master's degree in International Trade at ISEAD. After that, in 2011 he enrolled Arkadin, one of the top-2 provider for collaboration services worldwide, as the Sales Director for Spain and Portugal, and also started attending an Executive MBA at IESE Business School, one of the top-ranking business school focused on managers for large corporations and global management.

Since July 2012, Luis is the Country Manager for Spain in Podsystem, the only carrier providing flat free mobile Internet in Europe.

Along his professional life, Luis has founded three companies, including one engineering design firm and an online retailer for the e-book market. He speaks four languages and is the author of several books and numerous articles about social technology, business improvement through technology and related topics in international congresses and magazines.

Luis became Senior Member at IEEE in

Summer 2012. He is proud of bringing the complexity of technology to managers, business people and everyone in a very plain and understandable style, letting the people benefit from the latest trends in the market.

If you want to contact Luis, please write to aflores@ieee.org, or visit his website:

www.antonioflores.es.

www.ingramcontent.com/pod-product-compliance
Lightning Source LLC
Chambersburg PA
CBHW022124170526
45157CB00004B/1739